PAINSWICK

TIME CHART OF A COTSWOLD VILLAGE

Painswick Church.

PAINSWICK

TIME CHART OF
A COTSWOLD VILLAGE

by

CARL MORELAND F.R.G.S.

Carl Moreland.

Published by Carl Moreland
in association with
The Painswick Local History Society

I summon up remembrance of things past . . .
   SHAKESPEARE *Sonnet* NO. XXX

. . . I prayed for a plot of land, not so very large, containing a garden; and near the homestead a spring of fresh water, and a stretch of woodland to complete it.
   HORACE 65–8 BC

And on an English home—grey twilight poured
On dewy pastures, dewy trees,
Softer than sleep—all things in order stored
A haunt of ancient peace.
   TENNYSON

First published 1996

© 1996 by Carl Moreland

All rights reserved. No part of this publication may be
reproduced in any form or by any means—graphic, electronic
or mechanical, including photocopying, recording, taping
or information storage and retrieval systems—without
prior permission of the publishers.

ISBN 0 9528214 0 0 (Paperback)
ISBN 0 9528214 1 9 (Hardback)

Typeset in 12pt Monotype Bembo (270) (Hot Metal), 2pt leaded
by Gloucester Typesetting Services, Stonehouse GL10 3RG
Printed and bound by
Bookcraft, Midsomer Norton, Bath, Avon

Copyrights:
Text—Carl Moreland
Sketches—Zoë Greenwell
Map—John Bailey

Cover Illustration:
A glimpse of New Street, Painswick
painted about 1975 by Donald H. Edwards

Frontispiece:
Painswick Church, *c.* 1890,
soon after the spire was rebuilt.

Sketches of the buildings in
the Rococo Garden by kind permission
of Lord Dickinson

CONTENTS

Acknowledgements	9
Introduction	11
Map of Painswick *c.* 1500	*facing* 20
Time Chart	24
Glossary	55
Bibliography	59
Index	60
Colophon	64

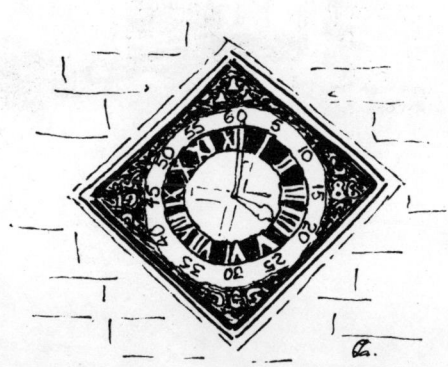

PART OF THE EAGLE HOUSE
ROCOCO GARDEN

ACKNOWLEDGEMENTS

John Speed, the famous cartographer, in the introduction to his Atlas, *The Theatre of the Empire of Great Britaine*, published in 1611, wrote to his 'Gentle, well favoured reader' the following words:

> It may well be objected that I have laid my building on other men's foundations, as indeed, who can do otherwise in a subject of this nature.

These words are especially true of the history of Painswick which must always be linked with the names of W. St Clair Baddeley and Sir Francis Hyett whose books were published in the early part of this century. Reference is made to them at some length in the introductory chapter of the present work and the author acknowledges his debt to both of them and to others listed in the short bibliography.

He is also grateful to members of the Painswick Local History Society and to other friends in the village who have provided him with interesting details for inclusion in the chronological charts—and grateful, too, to the staff of Painswick Library who have become used to having a number of books out on almost permanent loan.

The map of the village (as we imagine it might have been 'once upon a time') was drawn by John Bailey and the splendid sketches, which enliven the pages were drawn by Zoë Greenwell of Cheltenham.

OLD TOWN HALL PAINSWICK

INTRODUCTION

Readers interested in the history of Painswick can be forgiven for asking whether another work on the subject—even a brief one—is really necessary. Of course, it is true that we already have two very serious, long established, books to refer to, but times change: style, perceptions of historical events, readers' knowledge and taste alter, gradually in the short term, but radically over half a century or more.

Our two major books of reference, the *History of Painswick* by W. St Clair Baddeley and *Glimpses of the History of Painswick* by Sir Francis Hyett, published in 1907 and 1928 respectively are works of great erudition, the result of an immense amount of research which would daunt all but the most dedicated historian. Indeed, without them, we would know very little of our history.

The present monograph is simply a distillation of their work plus notes from other sources, in particular from the *Victoria History of the County of Gloucester*. In looking at history in its broadest sense the writer always feels that facts and dates, however important in themselves, do not really mean very much, but take on a new perspective when set out in relation to other events of the time. After all, our village didn't exist in isolation—hence the idea of setting out the past in a chronological chart: history, perhaps in a more visual form than usual.

However, a layout in this columnar form does set a limit to the detail which can be shown, a shortcoming which some may well feel detracts from its value. Therefore, the following general notes in more conventional narrative form should be regarded as supplementary to the detail in the charts.

To go back to 'beginnings': it would be splendid to have clear evidence of the time when the village was founded but, alas, we have to resort to conjecture and guess-work. From the detail given in the Domesday Book in 1086 it can be estimated that the population then was probably between 250 and 300 and it is quite likely that the original settlement dated back some three or four centuries, even perhaps to Roman days for the remains of Ifold villa are only a short distance away. We can imagine a small group of farmers from, say, the lowlands along the Severn where their land was subject to constant flooding, deciding in desperation to 'take to the hills' and choosing a site where there was ample water, abundant woodland for fuel and building and good sheep country. Perhaps also, the confluence of two streams, a traditional site for building a first chapel or church influenced their choice. So, it became a settled community growing slowly over the years until by the eleventh century, as we show in the chart, the Manor of Wyke covered a very large area and formed part of the estates of the Saxon Ernisi family. After the Conquest, the Manor was awarded to the powerful de Laci family from Lassy/Lasci in Normandy, whose main properties were at Weobley in Herefordshire and at Ludlow. In all, the de Laci's held over 100 manors so it is unlikely that they ever spent much time in our village except, no doubt, for hunting or when journeying to and from Normandy.

Following the de Laci's, our Lords of the Manor included some of the most powerful men in the land, well known in the history of England—not always for very commendable reasons: two were executed, one probably murdered, one committed suicide, four were killed in battle, two killed accidentally and one, who was imprisoned in the Tower of London, was said to have died of joy on being released.

Our chart can give only the briefest outline of their lives but several of the early Lords of the Manor deserve greater attention. The succession from one family to another rarely passed directly but by complex relationships through second marriages of widows or the marriages of sons and daughters into other noble families of the time. Only a close reading of 'Baddeley' or 'Hyett' will reveal the full details as far as they are known.

The Lordship of the Manor passed in this way by marriage from the de Laci family to Pain Fitzjohn (who gave his name to the village) and later, through the marriage of his daughter Agnes to the Munchensis who, at that time (1203), were probably the most powerful and wealthy baronial family in the country. Warine de Munchensi (II) who was close to the King, left the sum of 200,000 marks, the equivalent of many millions of pounds today.

The Valence family were equally powerful, active in the baronial wars of the time, fighting on the King's side. William de Valence, half brother of Henry III, called himself Earl of Pembroke to which he had no title, although his wife was heiress to the Earldom. His son, Aymer de Valence was one of the most notable figures of his day as the brief notes in the chart illustrate. They, in turn, were succeeded by the Talbot family. In 1346, Richard, the 2nd Lord Talbot, fought at Crécy—one of nine knights from Gloucestershire said to have taken part in the battle—and then travelled to Avignon to seek permission from Pope Clement VI to found an Augustinian Priory at Flanesford, near Goodrich Castle in the Wye valley. In 1348, a grant of land at Segrym's Mill was made as part of the endowment of the new Priory.

Later, the most prominent of the Talbot family was John (c.1388–1453), created Earl of Shrewsbury in 1442. Apart from being 'Governor and Lieutenant of France' and 'Governor of Ireland', he is said to have fought in no less than forty battles in France including taking part in the siege of Orleans against the French, then under the spell of Joan of Arc. There, he was captured and held by the French for three years, eventually being ransomed by the King. Shakespeare's Henry IV tells some of the story. In 1453 he was killed with his eldest son, the first Lord Lisle, again fighting in France but our special interest in him lies in a document drawn up on the 21st April c.1442/3 reading 'at which Courte [at Painswick] came Lord Talbot, his owne person...' its purpose to set up an 'Inqueste' of twenty local men from the four village tithings, to rule upon all matters and complaints affecting the relationship between the Lord of the Manor and his tenants: especially to consider the grievances of the widows of eleven local men slain in the French wars (out of sixteen who served with Lord Talbot). These widows would by custom lose their land holdings on the death of their husbands. It was ruled that 'they should have their livings and marry with whom they liste' and that inheritance could be through the female line. The findings of the Court setting out these

'Customs of the Manor' were remarkably generous and benevolent for their time and are detailed in Baddeley's history, making fascinating reading. In later times the 'Customs' were brought up to date in 1613 and were ratified by Act of Parliament in 1624, a rare event for so small a village.

Soon after the death of Lord Talbot and his son (the 1st Viscount Lisle) in battle in 1453, the complex quarrel with the Berkeley family which had drifted on through several generations finally came to a head. At one stage (1452), Berkeley Castle had been 'captured' and looted by the de Lisles: subsequent litigation failed to placate either party. Eventually, in 1469, the young Lord Lisle (the 2nd Viscount) unwisely challenged the Berkeleys to settle the issue and in the ensuing 'battle' at Nibley Green (in which one account says there were 2,000 combatants, a most unlikely figure) Lord Lisle was killed. Even after this drastic outcome, law suits continued and were not settled until 1609! It is of interest to note that this so called 'battle' was the last of its kind between rival families on English soil.

After the death of the 4th Viscount Lisle (1504), the Lordship of the Manor had a chequered history for half a century with such figures as Thomas Cromwell, Sir William Kingston and the infamous Sir Anthony Kingston appearing briefly on the scene as our Chart shows, the Manor eventually passing by marriage to the Jerningham family from Norfolk who remained here until the nineteenth century.

In contrast to the quite detailed knowledge we have of our early

Our Englysshe commodytees wolle and tynne (1436)

Lords of the Manor, especially where they were national figures, we know comparatively little about the daily lives of our villagers.

Agriculture in its various forms was, of course, all important in the fight for survival. From very early days, possibly even from Roman times, 'an open' field system operated with rotation between corn crops and fallow, each villager, according to rank, tilling a number of strips of the Lord's land. At the time of the Domesday Survey the number of plough teams in Gloucestershire

BARTERING WOOL FOR CLOTH

BARTERING WHEAT FOR WOOL

was over 3,800 (fifty-three in Painswick) each working 100/120 acres, giving a greater area under plough than today. In the same Survey we are told there were four mills in the village, a necessary part of food production.

At the same time sheep farming provided not only food and clothing but also the prospect of wealth. In the eleventh, twelfth and thirteenth centuries, for the most part a time of prosperity and rising population, England exported great quantities of wool, much of which came from the Cotswolds. Around the year 1300, the Abbot of Gloucester is said to have had flocks of some 10,000 sheep which produced forty-six sacks of wool each year: similar quantities were produced by the Berkeley family and other great landlords.

Unhappily, their prosperity was not to last: late in the thirteenth century climatic change brought very long cold periods to the British Isles and Northern Europe with consequent widespread famines, and in 1349/50 the Black Death devastated the lands. These misfortunes, compounded by acute labour shortage in England and by wars on the Continent, were to have a happy result for this country in driving many families of Flemish weavers to find a more settled life here. Although the export of untreated wool was in decline after the Black Death nevertheless England exported about 30,000 sacks a year in 1350/60 and, in 1397 one Tuscan trader alone imported 39,000 lbs of English wool through Genoa. At the same time he imported quantities of high quality English cloth bought by his Italian agents in London. His accounts show that these agents travelled widely in East Anglia and the Cotswolds and bid at auctions at 'Norleccio' (Northleach), 'Boriforte' (Burford), and the abbey at 'Siricestri' (Cirencester). During the next centuries the export of wool declined still further, but the manufacture of finished cloth became a major industry with our own local mills playing an increasing part. As is well known, the industry was all important until the first quarter of the nineteenth century in providing employment and sufficient wealth to create the splendid village architecture and array of millhouses, unique, even in the Cotswolds. But, as always in human affairs, change in trading conditions and recessions, even then, took their toll.

The great demand for uniform material during the years of the Napoleonic Wars faded after 1815 and, at the same time, competition from the Northern mill towns with their power-driven spinning machinery became ever fiercer—so much so that by the 1820's and 1830's the local woollen industry was in long-term decline. In 1830, a time of great unrest in the country generally, it is recorded that serious rioting took place in the town and a party of ten dragoons from Dursley was called in 'to assist the constables'. Although the precise cause of the rioting is not known there can be little doubt that a primary cause, if not the only one, was the

> Softe wolle she wroughte To kepe hire (her) from slouthe & idilnesse.
> Chaucer c. 1385

> Liberte for certayn cottesolde shepe to be transported unto the countre of Spayne.
> Halle Chronicles 1548

dissatisfaction among the local cloth makers at their loss of livelihood and the gloomy prospects for the future. Many mills did turn to other trades such as saw milling, brewing and pin making but these could never fully take the place of the old industry.

Whilst Painswick was being transformed architecturally at the time of its greatest prosperity in the seventeenth and eighteenth centuries, so also was the countryside, not always to the benefit of the farming world. Indeed, by the year 1800, agriculture was in decline with fewer and fewer employed on the land and farm wages were less than half those in the wool trade. The reasons were not far to seek: in the sixteenth and early part of the seventeenth centuries, the movement towards land enclosure which then occurred at the whim of landowners became subject to legislation and one of the earliest local Acts of Parliament was in 1668. In the next century the movement gained momentum and, as early as 1703 there are clear indications that most of the land in the parish had been enclosed. Throughout that century the effect of numerous Acts of Parliament, until about 1830, finally brought to an end the ancient system of communal farming and formed the landscape we know today.

THE RED HOUSE
ROCOCO GARDEN

To come for a moment much nearer to our own times, it is interesting to recall memories of the Arts and Crafts Movement, based largely in the Cotswolds, which touched our village life from the turn of the nineteenth century; indeed, even today its influence persists.

The Movement arose in the second half of the nineteenth century in reaction against the mass production of the Industrial Revolution. A small group led by William Morris turned to methods of craftsmanship of earlier days and hoped to persuade new generations to look at manufacturing furniture, textiles, jewellery and the like with a new perspective. For a few years their influence was widespread but they were too impractical to make headway against the industrial trends of the time, and eventually the Movement was confined to a small dedicated 'brotherhood' in this part of the world where, more than anywhere else, traditional craftsmanship had survived.

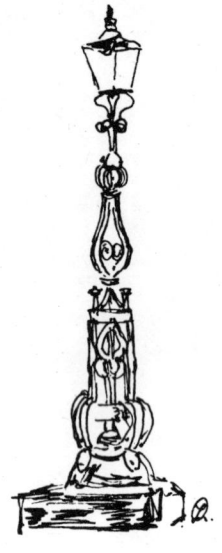

In Painswick, or nearby, their architectural imprint was unmistakeable. The Institute, the Gyde Almshouses and Orphanage, Little Fleece, the Bath-house, the War Memorial, the Lamp, Painswick Lodge, Hilles (Harescombe) and other properties were either built, extended, or altered, by Sidney Barnsley, W. Curtis Green, Detmar Blow, Sir George Oakley and others, often adorned with Eric Gill's characteristic inscriptions in beautiful lettering. Apart from buildings, there are examples in village houses of furniture made by Ernest Gimson and the Barnsley family, and of handblock printed textiles made at Hambutts House in the 1930's by Phyllis Barron and Dorothy Larcher, whose work was in great demand until the outbreak of the Second World War. Later, Phyllis Barron played a prominent part in the Gloucestershire Guild of Craftsmen, whose annual exhibitions in the village still bear the imprint of the Arts and Crafts Movement.

It would not be fitting to end this short introduction to our history without some reference to local events at the time of the Civil War which must have left a trail of distress and loss to the people of the village and its surroundings.

About 1640, in the Painswick tithings, Edge, Spoonbed, Sheepscombe, and Stroud-end there were between 150 and 200 families, a total population of some 600/800 people, a stable community with a steadily increasing prosperity based on the wool trade and agriculture, rarely disturbed by the outside world. Villagers could scarcely have imagined that they would ever be at the centre of a Civil War between King and Parliament and that on two occasions the King himself would be seen in or near, the village.

The first hint that unusual influences might be at work came in the 1630's when ecclesiastical tensions between traditionalists and puritans led to the rejection in 1640 of a vicar of Painswick by order of Parliament and later, when the war had started, feelings in the village ran so high that his successor was violently removed.

The first skirmishes of the war were fought in the Midland counties but by 1643 the action had moved much nearer with the capture of Bristol and Cirencester by the Royalists and in August 1643 the King reached Painswick to command the siege of Gloucester. He is said to have spent the nights of 9th August and 5th September at the Court House: this may have been so, but it is more likely that he chose The Lodge, the seat of the Lord of the Manor, occupied at that moment by Sir Ralph Dutton, an ardent Royalist, who was the garrison commander at Cirencester. However that may be, the King issued a Proclamation 'at our Court at Painswick' on the 10th August regarding 'victualling' the Army, detailing punishments to be meted out for malpractice in dealing with village people.

Gloucester was besieged, unsuccessfully, from the 10th August to 5th September, when the threat of attack by Parliamentary forces from the Cheltenham direction caused the Royalists to lift the siege. After breaking camp, they spent the night on the Beacon in '... most miserable, tempestuous, rainy weather ...' until '... the "creasing" winds the next morning dried up our thorough wet clothes ...'. The scene may be imagined all too clearly.

However, this was not the end of the war for Painswick. Early in the next year, 1644, Prince Rupert billeted some 2,000 men in the village and the surrounding area demanding contributions from the rich clothiers and others. Their presence here provoked sporadic and not very successful forays from the Cromwellian forces in Gloucester but eventually the Royalists withdrew temporarily to Tewkesbury. A month or two later, Cromwellian troops descended on the village and, they, too, demanded contributions for their cause. In subsequent fighting, the Church was badly damaged by fire and 'hand grenadoes' and the Kingston tomb and others were desecrated. Thereafter, the fighting moved away from the village although there were probably many skirmishes in the area. The last battle of the Civil War was fought near Stow on the Wold in March 1646.

Although the war was so close to home, we know little of the involvement of village people in the fighting—some must have been supporters of the Royalist cause, others Cromwellian which no doubt left a long legacy of bitterness between families and we may imagine the disturbance caused to a small community by the passage of so many armed men, frequently ill-disciplined, rarely paid and badly fed.

On the theme of wars in general we also know all too little of their effect on village life over the centuries. As already recorded, we do know that, of the sixteen Painswick men who served in France with Lord Talbot about the year 1440, eleven were killed and this cannot have been an isolated event. There are very occasional references which give us some help. A detailed record of 1608 shows that of 167 men in the village, twenty-one were trained as 'pykemen' or were able to use a musket or a caliver (a light musket) and many possessed a corslet or cuirass (body armour). Later, in 1684 there is a note in the magistrates records that 'there is due to John Gyde for his soldiers' pay, £30. 4. 6.'; in 1693 the magistrates gave 'two maimed soldiers 8*d*. and four more 1*s*. 8*s*.' and in 1695 'gave to 12 soldiers taken at Brest by the French, 2*s*.' The seventeenth, eighteenth and nineteenth centuries saw a score of wars on the Continent and, of course, in America, India and Africa, in which, no doubt Painswick men fought—and died. One reason for the first census in 1801 was to reveal the number of men who might 'volunteer' or be called upon to serve in the war with France at that time and it is believed that in 1815, or maybe a year or two later, Frith Wood was replanted with saplings from the field of Waterloo to celebrate Wellington's victory. Was it also, perhaps, a memorial to Painswick men who may have taken part in the battle?

In our own time the war memorials in Painswick, Edge and Sheepscombe testify that, in the Great War of 1914–18, no less than sixty-nine men failed to return to their families and in the Second World War a further twenty men gave their lives.

Perhaps the present war memorial may also serve as a reminder of the thirty generations of villagers who have lived here in the long centuries since the Norman Conquest and who have made the same sacrifices.

THE LYCHGATE

> The wonder of the world
> The beauty and the power,
> The shapes of things,
> Their colours, lights and shades:
> These I saw.
> Look ye also while life lasts.
> *Anon*

Page 22: Detail from Christopher Saxton's map of Gloucestershire published in his 'Atlas of England and Wales' in 1579. Cotswold appears as 'Cotes Wowlde'.

Page 23: Detail from John Speed's map of Gloucestershire published in his 'Theatre of the Empire of Great Britaine' in 1610/11. Yet another form of Coteswold—'Coteswovld'.

PAINSWICK

TIME CHART OF A COTSWOLD VILLAGE

... Believe me noble Lord
I am a stranger heere in Gloucestershire.
These high wild hilles, and rough uneven waies
Drawes out our miles, and makes them wearisome
   Shakespeare RICHARD II

In Europe the best wool is English
In England the best wool is Cotswold
   A popular medieval saying

... an house of hewn stone, in a fine situation
and a very pretty garden
   Bishop Pocock, a visit to Painswick House 1757

[24]

ROMAN AND SAXON ENGLAND

It takes only a short walk to the top of the Painswick Beacon to remind us that, several thousand years ago, our remote ancestors constructed the great defensive ramparts for protection against wolves and hostile neighbours. We can only guess at the way of life of these people, perhaps as hunters, shepherds or pig breeders, and not until the Romans over-ran this part of the country about the year AD 60 do we find historical evidence to tell us how people really lived.

We all know of the Roman presence in Gloucestershire, of Corinium, the second city in England, of Glevum, the fortified city guarding the River Severn crossing and of Chedworth, a typical 'manor house' of the time. Although it seems unlikely that there was a Roman settlement in the area of the village itself, the remains of the third century villa at Ifold are not too far away and, of course, there may well be others, undiscovered. The sight of travellers between Cirencester and Gloucester journeying perhaps via Bisley must have been common enough, seemingly part of a permanent way of life. But, in the year 410, after eleven or twelve generations of Roman rule—relatively benign and secure in our part of England—the world our villagers knew changed and began the slow decline into four centuries of turmoil and unrest: the threat of Saxon invasion, culminating in the battle at Dyrham and the capture of Bath, Cirencester and Gloucester, the everlasting quarrels and wars between Wessex and Mercia and, later, the Viking invasions. Moreover the four terrible plagues of 664–683, decimated the population. Perhaps not the 'Dark Ages' which we tend to imagine, but certainly the beneficent influence of Rome, its order, its speech, towns and institutions vanished, leaving a vacuum to be filled by the strongest hand.

Apart from the arrival of St Augustine and the spread of Christianity there was to be little or no enlightenment (except in Northumbria) until the end of the ninth century in the time of Alfred (871–899) and his immediate successors under whose rule the Danes were at last kept in check. It was in this period that our 'shires' acquired their first vague shape arising out of a unification of the old land divisions—the hundreds

—brought together under the protection of the larger garrison towns to which a levy had to be rendered. The shire of Gloucester took its present form—more or less—in 1017 when it combined with the shire of Winchcombe. (The word 'county' was introduced in later years by the Normans). Sometime in these long centuries a few English or Saxon families must have grouped together to form a settled community on the site of our village, clearing the woodland to build timber-framed houses and to make way for crops and animals.

To read accounts of these times one would imagine that life was in constant turmoil but probably villagers' life changed very little unless they were unfortunate enough to be over-run by warring factions or to be dragooned into military service. Practically all 'ordinary' people who made up 95 per cent or more of the total were employed on the land or in work associated with it—an agricultural society in which villagers' lives and routine were bound by complex but long-established and accepted rules giving a sense of security to community life. Their loyalty was to their superior or 'lord', the Church and to the community in clearly defined terms.

The Domesday survey gives us an idea of these social divisions, some of which may well have survived since pre-Roman times. Although customs varied greatly in different parts of the country our thirty-five villeins (or 'gebur') probably lived in timber-framed houses and had a strip or strips of land and animals provided for them by the local 'lord' for whom they worked perhaps three to four days a week on average: the other days they worked for themselves or to pay Church dues. The bordars (smallholders) had rather less land and rendered even more service to their lord; the eleven slaves were the bottom rung but they were allocated a strip of land and had some freedom to sell their own surplus produce—if they were fortunate. The riding-men (or radknights) must have been specially chosen for their duties as escorts to the Lord of the Manor or whoever their superior may have been and no doubt they also served as carriers or news-bearers between communities. Finally, we have our Priest and presumably therefore, a church, of which unfortunately we know so little. One or two Norman remains have been found on the present site and there seems no reason to doubt that a Saxon or Norman church existed. Maybe it was like other Cotswold churches such as those at Duntisbourne Rous or Elkstone but that we shall probably never know.

HISTORICAL BACKGROUND	KINGS AND QUEENS
c.60–400 Roman Period	
c.500–600 Saxon Invasions	
577 Battle of Dyrham. The Saxons capture Bath, Cirencester and Gloucester	
597 Mission of Saint Augustine	
c.600–700 Gloucester formed part of the Kingdom of Hwicce	
679 Founding of St Peter's Monastery at Gloucester	757–796 Offa, King of Mercia
c.790 First Viking Raids	827–839 Egbert, King of all England
877–879 Viking raiders occupied Gloucester and Cirencester	871–899 Alfred, King of Wessex
	899–924 Edward, the Elder
940 Athelstan died at Gloucester, buried at Malmesbury	924–940 Athelstan, King of all England
c.1015 Second wave of Viking invaders	1017–1035 Cnut, Viking King of England
	1042–1066 Edward the Confessor

[27]

Historical Background	Kings and Queens	Lords of the Manor
	1042–1066 Edward the Confessor	c.1050 Ernisi (the Elder) held the manor-part of his estates of possibly 30/40,000 acres
1066 Norman Conquest	1066–1087 William I	c.1070 Walter de Laci (of Lassy in Normandy). Fought at Battle of Hastings. Founder of St Peter's Abbey in Hereford, accidentally killed there
1085–1086 Domesday Survey commissioned in Gloucester 1089 Building of Abbey Church of St Peter in Gloucester began	1087–1100 William II	1085 Roger de Laci As a supporter of Robert of Normandy's claim to the throne he was banished in 1096 for rebellion
1095–1291 The Crusades	1100–1135 Henry I	c.1100 Hugh de Laci It is recorded that he was a 'palmer', i.e. had been on a crusade to the Holy Land. In about 1118 he granted the advowson of the Church to the Priory of Llanthony Prima which he had founded (c.1108). The Manor passed by marriage of his niece to

[In the year 1051, Earl Godwin rebelled against Edward the Confessor and raised an army at Beverstone Castle (Tetbury) intending to attack the King at Gloucester. Folklore tells us that Godwin camped on the Beacon before attacking, hence the traditional use of the name, 'Castle Godwin']	1135–1154
	Stephen
		1121
		Pain Fitzjohn
		Sheriff of Shropshire and Hereford—killed in a skirmish with the Welsh. Succeeded by his daughter:
		1137
		Cecilia Fitzjohn
		who held it for sixty-five years.
		Married: I Earl of Hereford
		         II William of Poitou
		         III Walter of Mayenne
		Having no children, the Manor passed to her sister, Agnes

LLANTHONY ABBEY

CHURCH, BUILDINGS, ROADS, LANDSCAPE	VILLAGE LIFE AND EVENTS

In the earliest times the village was named Wyke, Wicke or Wykeham [Latin, Vicus = Old English Wyke/Wic = a village or dwelling]

Wyke, in the Hundred of Bisley, recorded as one of the largest manors in the County—about 20,000 acres consisting of some 14,000 acres of woodland and 6,000 arable. It was divided into four Tithings—Spoonbed, Edge, Stroud-end and Sheepscombe with a complex system of land measurement of which 'a virgate' was the basis:
  Virgate (yard-land)=
    about 30 acres
  Hide—2 to 4 virgates=
    60–120 acres

Domesday Book records:
  Woodlands: 5 leagues × 2, worth £24.
  4 working mills 'rendering' 24 sh.
  53 teams of oxen.
  66 male inhabitants including:
    35 villeins (tenant farmers)
    16 bordars (small holders)
    3 radknights (escorts to the Lord of the Manor)
    11 serfs (slaves)
    1 priest.
[An estimated total population of, say, 250/300]

c.1100–1150
Probably a Manor House on the site of Castle Hale and the Court House. It may have been fortified by Pain Fitzjohn or his successors and later was known as a 'Castellum'. Later still, c.1550, recorded as 'Castle Halle'

c.1150
The advowson of the Church passed to the Priory of Llanthony Secunda in Gloucester (founded in 1136)

At this time the village name became 'Wyke Pagani' or 'Paynes-wyke' and later still 'Painswick'.
  There is no written record of it in this form until c.1237 and c.1265

[29]

Historical Background	Kings and Queens	Lords of the Manor
	1154–1189 Henry II	
	1189–1199 Richard I	
1215 Magna Carta	1199–1216 John	c.1203 Agnes Fitzjohn Married into the Munchensi family: the Manor passed to Warine de Munchensi I c.1204 William de Munchensi I c.1205 Warine de Munchensi II
1216 Henry III crowned in the Abbey at Gloucester In these times the units of currency in general use were the silver penny (a groat) = 4*d*. and there were 2*d*., 1*d*., ½*d*. and ¼*d*. pieces. Pounds and shillings (and the mark = 13 sh/4*d*.) were only used for accounting purposes—there were no equivalent coins in circulation	1216–1272 Henry III 1272–1307 Edward I	According to the historian Matthew Paris of St Albans: 'one of the noblest and wisest barons of England' 1255 William de Munchensi II Fought with Simon de Montfort against the King at Lewes and Kenilworth; consequently dispossessed and the Manor was claimed by: 1266 William de Valence Known as the Earl of Pembroke, he was half-brother of Henry III 1279 William de Munchensi II The Manor was restored to him by Edward I. He was killed in the Welsh Wars
1295 Meeting of the 'Model Parliament'		1289 Joan de Munchensi Widow of William de Valence

Church, Buildings, Roads, Landscape	Village Life and Events
Until the middle of the fifteenth century the Lords of the Manor probably used the old Manor House on the site of Castle Hale as a residence during their visits to Painswick but, after that building was demolished about 1450, the Lodge, set in the hunting park, became the Manor House until 1835	The Conquest brought little change in the way of life in communities such as Painswick, although nationally it was a time of increasing prosperity. Life was still based on agricultural products—cereals, cattle, sheep, wool, timber and, no doubt quarrying on the Beacon to meet the needs of the time
	c.1220 'Miscreants came by night to the house of Geoffrey, son of Godwin of Wyke and killed him, his wife and all his family. It is not known whom they were'. (The village would face a daily fine until the criminals were caught.)
c.1250 Probably a house on the site of the Lodge about this time	1253 Charter granted for a weekly market
1263 Sheepscombe taking shape as a separate settlement	
	1277 Roger Loveday appointed custodian of William de Munchensi's lands during Munchensi's exile
1291 The 'vicarage' was worth £7	

Historical Background	Kings and Queens	Lords of the Manor
In Northern Europe the years from 1280 to 1350 were blighted by a mini 'Ice Age' and famines were frequent and severe	1307–1327 Edward II	1296 Ay(l)mer de Valence, Earl of Pembroke Known as 'Guardian of Scotland'. Defeated Robert Bruce in 1307. Fought at Bannockburn. Died in a tournament at Compiegne near Paris in 1324. Buried in Westminster Abbey
		c.1324 Elizabeth Comyn Niece of Aymer de Valence was forcibly 'usurped' by Hugh Dispenser the Elder who took over the Manor. In 1326 she was 'rescued' by Richard, Lord Talbot who married her, thereby becoming Lord of the Manor
1327 Edward II murdered in Berkeley Castle: buried in the Abbey at Gloucester	1327–1377 Edward III	
c.1346 Battle of Creçy. Nine knights from Gloucestershire fought in the battle		1326 Richard Lord Talbot Founded Augustinian Priory at Flanesford in the Wye valley. The priory building still stands
1348–1350 Black Death		
		1356 Gilbert 3rd Baron Talbot
1378 Parliament assembled at Gloucester	1377–1399 Richard II	
		1387 Richard 4th Baron Talbot
	1399–1413 Henry IV	1396 Gilbert 5th Baron Talbot In 1404 fought the Welsh under Owen Glendower. Succeeded by his 2-year-old daughter, Ankaret, d. 1421
	1413–1422 Henry V	
1415 Battle of Agincourt		

Church, Buildings, Roads, Landscape	Village Life and Events
c.1300 The names 'Coteswaud'—'Coddeswold'—'Coteswolde' coming into use	c.1300 Long before the first mention of the village wool trade (c.1440) sheep rearing was a great source of wealth. In 1300, the Abbot of Gloucester is said to have had flocks of 10,000 sheep
1314 The Castle (Castle Hale) recorded as worth three shillings and four pence p.a., 60 acres of arable land at six shillings p.a. and other pasture and woodland	1314 Thomas, Lord Berkeley and forty supporters 'riotously entered Painswick Park' and stole all the deer. Subsequently defied the coroners, but were pardoned by the King in return for military service
	1321 Lord of the Manor granted a further Charter for a weekly market and annual fair
1327 Record of land farmed by the Damsell family	1327 Sixty-eight villagers assessed as tax payers
1348 A grant of fields (above Seagrimsbridge) was made to Flanesford	
1350–1400 The 'Chur', 'Little Fleece' and other houses in the High Street (Bisley Street) built in this period. Later rebuilt in seventeenth and eighteenth centuries	
1377–1401 Present Church being built	
1413 Sale of a mill called 'Ludlowes' (Brookhouse Mill)	1398 In return for a loan of 100 marks Richard II gave leave to the Prior of Llanthony Abbey to incorporate the Vicarage of Painswick (taxed 10 marks) to hold for his own use in perpetuity
1415 Land owned by John Damsel transferred to Llanthony Abbey	

[33]

Historical Background	Kings and Queens	Lords of the Manor
	1422–1461 Henry VI	c.1421 John 6th Baron Talbot. In 1442 created Earl of Shrewsbury, Governor and Lieutenant of France, Governor of Ireland. Killed with his son in battle in France. In 1442/3 held an 'Inqueste' in the village to clarify the 'Customs of the Manor'
1450 Invention of moveable type printing		1453 Thomas 2nd Viscount Lisle The Manor valued at £20 in his time. Killed at Nibley Green
1455–1485 Wars of the Roses	1461–1483 Edward IV	
		1469 Margaret, widow of Viscount Lisle
		c.1475 Edward Grey, 3rd Viscount Lisle
1489 The first £1 coin—a gold sovereign—was minted	1483 Edward V	
1492 Columbus to the New World	1483–1485 Richard III 1485–1509 Henry VII	c.1492 John, 4th Viscount Lisle After his death (1504) the Manor passed an uncertain period through Elizabeth Countess of Devon and her husbands: I. Sir Edmund Dudley II. Sir Arthur Plantagenet (d. 1510) Viscount Lisle—son of Edward IV In 1542 accused of conspiring to surrender Calais; imprisoned in the Tower, then pardoned by the King but 'expired of joy on hearing the newes'. In 1539 sold the Manor for £400 to Thomas Cromwell

Church, Buildings, Roads, Landscape

Village Life and Events

1429
A 'wateringhole' recorded at Horse pools.
Mention of 'New Hall', New Street, High Street (Bisley Street) and Barnet Street (Gloucester Street)

1430
Mention of land called 'Ham-butts', i.e. the area in Ham/m 'abutting' the Lord's land

1430
Prices fixed by Court Steward: chicken 3*d*., dove 1*d*., ½ goat 5*d*., 2 gals. milk 2*d*., 6 gals. beer 1 sh.

1439
Salmon's Mill recorded

c.1450
The Old Castle (Castle Hale) demolished about this time.
The village of Stroud, formerly part of Bisley parish, growing in importance as a centre of the wool trade

c.1440
Of sixteen Painswick men who served in France eleven were killed

1469
'Battle' at Nibley Green between the Talbots and the Berkeleys, the culmination of a prolonged quarrel between the families

1478
House now used as the Post Office built

1480
Church nave and tower built

1487
Statute of Henry VII
It is ordered that none shall have ale to sell without licence of the ale-tasters: fine 6 sh. 8*d*.

[35]

Historical Background	Kings and Queens	Lords of the Manor
1498 Vasco de Gama to India		
	1509–1547 Henry VIII	
1536 William Tyndale Translator of the Bible. Probably born at Slimbridge (c.1494). Burnt at the stake in Antwerp for heresy		1539 Thomas Cromwell, Earl of Essex, Secretary to Cardinal Wolsey, Chancellor of the Exchequer. Accused of treason and executed without trial. Manor passed to the Crown and thence to 1540 Sir William Kingston, Constable of the Tower of London. Buried in the Church. Manor passed to 1540 Sir Anthony Kingston. Said to have lived at Sheephouse and The Lodge. Conspired to depose Queen Mary but plot was discovered and Sir Anthony arrested; died, probably by his own hand, *en route* to London to stand trial (1556)
1540 Dissolution of the Monasteries. Llanthony Abbey suppressed 1541 Formation of Bishopric of Gloucester. The Abbey designated a Cathedral		
1555 Bishop Hooper burnt at the stake in Gloucester	1547–1553 Edward VI 1553–1558 Queen Mary	1556 Sir Henry Jerningham I of Costessy in Norfolk acquired the Manor through his wife Frances, niece of Anthony Kingston. A member of a powerful Catholic family, he was influential in securing the throne for Queen Mary. Knighted and appointed Captain of the Royal Guard. Fell from favour after the Queen's death

Church, Buildings, Roads, Landscape	Village Life and Events

1496
Rent roll of this year records seven mills including Kings Mill and Skinners Mill. Also Thomas Pytte holds one mess(uage) [dwelling house and meadow], 1 virgate [30 acres] called The Castle [Castle Hale], and 2 lundinates [?8 acres] at 23 sh. 11d. In all the following tenants with land are recorded in the Tithings:

		Rent
Strode-end	25	£21. 9. 11½
Egge	41	28. – 12(?)
Sponebed	24	14. 18. 11½
Shepescombe	14	8. 8. 2½

1535
The vicarage valued at £14. 15. 1½

1546–1547
Church Sanctuary and High Altar being built. Parish registers date from this time

1549
Sheephouse and meadow (rent 20 sh.) 'detained', apparently without authority by Sir Anthony Kingston

1554
An inn—with bowling green and cockpit—built on the site of the Falcon about this time

Before the 'new' road was made in 1818 the way to Stroud was via Stamages Lane—see below: c.1608—and at that time it was recorded as a 'Via Regia'—Kings Highway.

It is more than likely that this road was known from ancient times as 'the street to Wick', i.e. Wyke, the original Saxon name for the village

1496
Population: 118 families

1512
Henry Loveday recorded as a cloth maker

1535
Henry VIII and Anne Boleyn reputedly stayed at The Lodge for hunting whilst visiting Gloucester

1541
Statute of Henry VIII
It is ordered that none shall wash clothes or any other thing in the 'upper flowe' at Towys (Tobyes) well: fine 20d.

c.1550
The Lord of the Manor set up and 'endowed' a gallows at Sheepscombe with an executioner—and a 'prison' in Painswick

Historical Background	Kings and Queens	Lords of the Manor

	1558–1603 Elizabeth I	
		1572 Sir Henry Jerningham II
		The Jerningham family held the Manor until 1803 but, with one or two exceptions, they rarely lived at The Lodge. Some of their names are recorded in the Parish Registers
1581 Drake's circumnavigation of the world		
1588 The Armada		
1604 Gunpowder Plot	1603–1625 James I	
1606 Virginia Company founded		
		1619 Sir Henry Jerningham III Leased the Manor in 1636 to Sir Ralph Dutton at 20 sh. p.a. Dutton was an ardent Royalist who served with Prince Rupert: he led an assault on Bristol but later was forced to escape to France and was shipwrecked and drowned
1620 Sailing of the *Mayflower*		

Church, Buildings, Roads, Landscape	Village Life and Events
	1560 Sir Henry Jerningham continued to live in Norfolk and leased the Manor to Roger Lygon for £40 'by the yere'
	1563 142 households recorded
1566 Mention of Bulcross (a field name) near the Frith	**1576** The first record of a schoolmaster in the village
1579 Saxton's map of Gloucestershire records the name Cotes Wowlde	**1585** A labourer's wage recorded as 14d. (6p) a week
c.1600 A new Court House built by Thomas Gardner, clothier and Castle Hale being rebuilt by Thomas Pytte	**1596** 'A great dearth fell upon the land and there was much misery and poverty' (probably sheep murrain)
c.1601 Tocknells Mill	
c.1608 Thomas Stamage bought an acre of land from Castle Hale to build a house known as 'white walls' on the road to Wick Street (i.e. Stamages Lane)	**1607** William Motley named as the executioner at Sheepscombe and keeps the gallows, ladder and 'halter' in good repair
1610–1611 Speed's map of Gloucestershire now records the name Cotes Wovlde	**1608** Of 161 workers recorded, 47 were employed in the wool trade (4 clothiers, 33 weavers, 10 fullers), and there were 32 other traders and craftsmen
c.1620 Old Market Hall demolished to make way for cottages	
c.1622 The Cap Mill	**1622** Statute of James I It is ordered that none shall wash the entrails of swine at Tibby's Well—fine 6 sh. 8d.
c.1628–(1840) The Town Hall (the Stock House) incorporating a 'blind house' and school built 'outside the North Gate of the Cemetery'	

[39]

Historical Background	Kings and Queens	Lords of the Manor
	1625–1649 Charles I	The seventeenth century had started uneasily for the village. The Lord of the Manor attempted to impose restrictions of one kind or another on his tenants contrary to the Customs of the Manor set out in 1462; after much litigation the 'Customs' were confirmed by special Act of Parliament in 1624, a very rare event for so small a village.
1642–1648 Civil War		
1643 Cirencester and Bristol captured by the Royalists: the garrison in Cirencester commanded by Sir Ralph Dutton (of Painswick)		
1646 Last battle of the war fought near Stow-on-the-Wold		Thereafter, the quarrels between King and State, Church and Puritan, culminating in the Civil War brought much misery to the village, but happily, this was redeemed in the second half of the century by increasing prosperity in the wool trade, which, in later years was to transform the life of the village
	1649–1660 Cromwell	
1660 Royal Society founded	1660–1685 Charles II	1646 Sir Henry Jerningham IV
1666 Great Fire of London		
c.1680–(1830) Land Enclosure Acts		
1688 Bill of Rights	1685–1688 James II	1680 Sir Francis Jerningham

Church, Buildings, Roads, Landscape	Village Life and Events
1632 Church spire added	
1633 Wick Street House built	c.1636 Edward Seaman hanged for murder
1634 Painswick Mill recorded	1643 Siege of Gloucester
1600–1700 Edge House, Edge Hill Farm and other buildings round the green taking shape	Tradition holds that the King spent the nights of 9th August and 5th September in the village during the siege
	1644 Skirmishes in the village between Royalist and Cromwellian forces; the Church damaged by fire and tombs desecrated

	1650
	Population: 200 families. The Parish was policed by two constables:
	  1 for Edge and Spoonbed
	  1 for Sheepscombe and Stroud-end

1657–(1825) George Inn (in George Court) recorded: weekly markets probably held there	1657 Society of Friends meetings about this time.
c.1670 Lovedays Mill	1658–c.1771 The Friends Burial Ground at Dell Farm in use
c.1672 Fifty-two houses recorded in Sheepscombe tithing	1672 First meetings of Congregationalists
c.1674 Damsells Mill	1675 Thomas Twining born here—founded Twinings Tea House in the Strand: 1705/6
1680–1690 First church bells installed	
1684 A record of Twynings Mill 'at the crossing of the stream at the bottom of the stepping stones lane'. (Now Skinner's Mill)	1686 Society of Bellringers active until 1862
1694 Map of land owned by William Rogers of Castle Hale: survey by Stephen Jeffrey	1686–1691 A whipping post and ducking stool 'provided'

Historical Background	Kings and Queens	Lords of the Manor
c.1700–1800 Turnpike Acts	1689–1702 William and Mary	
	1702–1714 Queen Anne	
1707 Union with Scotland		
	1714–1727 George I	
1721–1742 Sir Robert Walpole—the first 'Prime Minister'		
	1727–1760 George II	1730 Sir John Jerningham Evidently lived for long periods at The Lodge as did his brother George who succeeded him 1737 Sir George Jerningham In his time the income from the Painswick estate was registered as £306. 11. 4¾d.
1749–1823 Edward Jenner Born and died at Berkeley: pioneer of smallpox vaccines. Lived for twenty years in Cheltenham where he gave vaccinations at 'The Pest House'		

Church, Buildings, Roads, Landscape | Village Life and Events

1700–1800
A century of great change and expansion, of building and re-building, during which Painswick grew from a village to a small town and assumed much of its present form. The population increased from about 186 families (say 600/700) to 3,150 at the first census in 1801. At the same time the Land Enclosure Acts changed the aspect of the countryside from the old strip system of cultivation to the hedged fields we see today.

1704–1725
First schools recorded

1705
First Congregational Chapel built

1706
Friends Meeting House built

c.1711
Present Falcon Inn built—probably on the site of earlier building; used as the meeting place for the Manor Court

1726
Gloucester–Painswick road improved under Turnpike Act

1733–1738
Building of Painswick House by Charles Hyett who moved from Gloucester to the 'good airs' of Painswick calling his house 'Buenos Ayres'. The house was built on the site of a farmhouse called 'Herings', an ancient copyhold estate

1733
A tollgate (the Barnet Street Turnpike) at Butt Green

c.1741
South aisle of Church built

c.1745
Rococo Garden laid out

c.1750
Pans Lodge built in Frith Wood (demolished sometime before 1824)

1700
Population—186 families:
    Stroud-end   48
    Spoonbed   33
    Shepscombe 33
    Edge   72
In the early part of the century the old weekly markets and annual fairs declined in importance but lingered on as sheep and cattle markets until 1879

1714 and 1741
Smallpox epidemics in the village

1716–1787
John Bryan, master mason, created many of the altar tombs in the churchyard

1737
Advert: 'The Cirencester Flying-Waggon' takes 3 days to London. From the Bull Inn (Wick Street) every Monday at 12 o'c. David Niblett, the Painswick carrier

1742
John Wesley preached in the village, the first of many visits

c.1750
Population said to be 2,256. Each tithing had an overseer of the poor

HISTORICAL BACKGROUND	KINGS AND QUEENS	LORDS OF THE MANOR
		1737 Sir George Jerningham
1754 James Hargreaves—invention of spinning Jenny		
1769 Richard Arkright—invention of water-powered spinning frame	1760–1820 George III	
1769–1789 James Watt—steam power		1774 Sir William Jerningham Active in Catholic emancipation movement. His house in Norfolk was a meeting place for exiled French nobility. He sold the Manor (excluding The Lodge) to Thomas Croome. In 1831 Sir William's grandson sold The Lodge and in 1836 most of it was demolished
c.1770–1830 Stage coaches		
1789 Severn/Thames canal via Sapperton tunnel opened. French Revolution		
1793–1815 Wars with France		
		1804 Thomas Croome
1805 Battle of Trafalgar		
1815 Battle of Waterloo		[Extract from *Gloucester Journal*, 16th March 1789: 'Our townsman Mr Bryan (nephew of John Bryan) is employed in paving anew the Royal Chapel at Windsor. After dinner at Windsor, the King came to view the work and said to Mr Bryan: "This is excellent stone that you bring from Painswick. Gloucester is a fine count(r)y and Painswick is one of the pleasantest places in the world" ']

Church, Buildings, Roads, Landscape	Village Life and Events

Church, Buildings, Roads, Landscape

c.1750–1760
High Street renamed Bisley Street

c.1750–1770
Yew trees planted

1751
First mention of Brookhouse Mill, previously known as 'Ludlowes'

c.1768
Beacon House

1781
Star Inn first mentioned

1784
First Sunday school opened

1800–1825
The peak of the village 'Industrial Age'—about thirty woollen mills working and weavers earned round 20 sh. a week

1805
Congregational Church built on site of earlier chapel

1808
Wesleyan Church built in New Street, later, in 1831, used by the Baptists

1818
A Savings Bank established for the Painswick area.
Stroud/Pitchcombe road opened.
Annual 'letting' of the Barton Street Turnpike at the Falcon Inn. Net takings £422 p.a.

Village Life and Events

1779
Advert: 'The Gloucester & Bath new and elegant Post Coach through Stroud and Painswick in just one day: Mondays and Thursdays. Inside passengers 11 sh. each'

1788–1808
Cornelius Winter—Minister of the Congregational Church

1788
George III travelled from Cheltenham via Birdlip, Painswick, Wick Street to Stroud

1800–1820
Agriculture in decline. Farm hands earned about 8 sh. a week, women 3 sh.
  Population:
    1801 – 3,150
    1811 – 3,201

1814
Samuel Jenner advertised his 'Flying Waggons to London from the Falcon Inn every Tuesday and Friday (via Wick Street)'

1820–1841
Thirteen Painswick 'felons' were transported to Australasia: three for life—but they probably died en route

Historical Background	Kings and Queens	Lords of the Manor
	1820–1830 George IV	
1825 First railway service—Stockton to Darlington		
1828–1831 First edition of the Ordnance Survey maps of this area		
		Population: 1821 – 4,044 1831 – 4,009 1841 – 3,734 1851 – 3,460 1861 – 3,229
1831 Gurney's Improved Patent Steam Coach ran three times daily from Gloucester to Cheltenham		
1832 Reform Acts	1830–1837 William IV	In 1837 the Lord of the Manor attempted unsuccessfully to assert his claim on the death of a tenant to his 'best quick beast' (the ancient law of heriot)
	1837–1901 Queen Victoria	1859 T. M. Croome

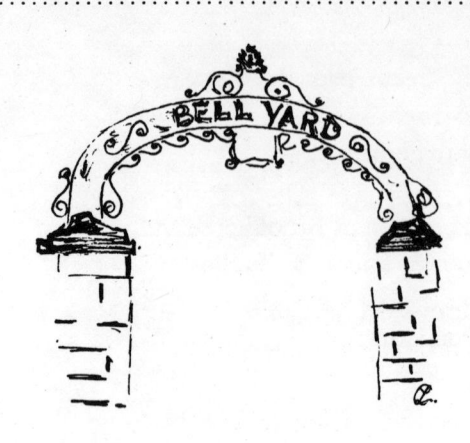

[46]

Church, Buildings, Roads, Landscape

Village Life and Events

1819
Stroud road extended to Painswick

1819–1820
Painswick/Brockworth road completed

1820–1840
Charles Baker of Castle Hale surveying and mapping in this period

1823
Cheltenham/Bath coaches advertised— daily from the Falcon

1820
Sheepscombe Church built

1825–1870
The village woollen industry in long-term decline. The inventions of the previous fifty years, steam power and spinning machinery, mass production in the northern cities and the fall in demand for uniforms after the Napoleonic wars brought to an end the cottage industry on which the village had depended for so many centuries.

1827–1832
Major additions to Painswick House by William Hyett

1830
Assembly Rooms built

1830
Serious unrest and rioting in the village; party of ten dragoons sent from Dursley 'to assist the constables'

1831
Mary Roberts of Yew Tree Cottage wrote 'Annals of my Village'

1832–(1991)
Burdocks building firm active

1832
William Hyett elected first MP for the new Stroud constituency

1838
Eight public houses and twenty-six beer shops recorded

1838
There were six emigrants to Australia (New South Wales)

1839
Charles Baker's revised large scale map is issued

1840
Old Town Hall (the Stock House) demolished. Present building erected in 'Pig Street'

1844
Sir Francis Hyett born

[47]

Historical Background	Kings and Queens	Lords of the Manor

1847
Stroud connected to main railway line to London

1837–1901
Queen Victoria

1856
Crimean War

1859
T. M. Croome

1866–c.1900
Proposals for Stroud/Painswick railway line

1870
Introduction of compulsory education

Population:
   1871 – 4,019
   1881 – 4,040
   1891 – 4,134
   1901 – 2,587*
   1911 – 2,638
   1921 – 2,488

1883
A. C. M. Croome

1890's–1950
Arts and Crafts Movement prominent in the South Cotswolds, including Sapperton and Painswick

1901–1910
Edward VII

* Boundaries adjusted

Church, Buildings, Roads, Landscape

1847
National School built

1851
The stocks installed in present position

1854
Methodist Chapel built

1860–(1910)
Gas, Light and Coke Co. operated in Kings Mill Lane. Taken over by Stroud Gas Co.

1863
Cemetery laid out for 'inhabitants of Edge and Spoonbed tithings'

1866
Edge Church built. Separate parish formed in 1873

1872
'Verlands' built as vicarage

1876
'Pig Street' renamed 'Russell Street' until 1901—now Victoria Street

c.1876–1962
Pin manufacturing at Brookhouse Mill

1881
Gyde Trustees grant for lighting the town

1883
Church spire destroyed in storm—rebuilt within six months

1891
Golf course laid out.
There were sixteen alehouses and six beer shops

c.1893
Castle Hale (then the Vicarage) damaged by fire

Village Life and Events

1860–1870
Changes in demand for special woollen materials led to the closure of the last woollen mills

1872
Frederick Gyde died. Left a bequest to set up a Trust 'for the benefit of the town of Painswick'. In 1894, after the death of his brother, Edwin, a much larger sum was used to set up a further Trust, which was indeed a great benefit to the town

[49]

Historical Background	Kings and Queens	Lords of the Manor

1894
Formation of Parish Councils to replace the ancient 'Vestry Meetings'

1910–
1937
  George V

1914–1918
  Great War

1937
  Edward VIII

1939–1945
  Second World War

1937–
1952
  George VI

1929
  Detmar Blow

[50]

Church, Buildings, Roads, Landscape	Village Life and Events
1893 Town Hall gutted by fire	
1894 Until this year Painswick Parish extended to Stroud and included Merrywalks and Beeches Green	**1894** Edwin Gyde died
	1895 Society of Bellringers re-formed
1896 Oil lamps in Vicarage Street—water and drainage systems started	**1896** Horse-drawn fire engine brought into use. Walter Burdock, captain of the Fire Brigade. Horse-drawn omnibuses to Stroud and Cheltenham advertised
1901 Lych-gate built	
1906–1908 Rev. W. Seddon enlarged the old house 'Gwynfa', his Vicarage (now Painswick Hotel) and made the 'New Drive' to the main road	**1897** Revival of Clipping Ceremony
1906 Mains water and drainage completed	
1907 Institute built	**1907** First publication of 'A Cotteswold Manor' by W. St Clair Baddeley
1910 New Inn (St Mary Street) converted for use as Police Station	**1912** G.W.R. motor omnibuses to Stroud and Cheltenham advertised
1913 Gyde Almshouses built to design by Sydney Barnsley	**1914–1915** Party of sixty-five Belgian war refugees billetted locally
1916 Gyde Orphanage started—opened in 1921	
1924 Public Baths built, also to design by Barnsley	
1930's Electricity supply brought to the village. New housing in Canton Acre and Upper Washwell	**1928** Publication of 'Glympses of the History of Painswick' by F. A. Hyett

Historical Background	Kings and Queens	Lords of the Manor

		1939 Jonathan Blow

The War Memorials in the churches of Painswick, Edge and Sheepscombe record the names of eighty-nine men who were killed in the wars:
   69 in 1914–18
   20 in 1939–45
		Population:
		  1931 – 2,542
		  1951 – 2,757
		  1961 – 2,844
		  1971 – 2,785
		  1981 – 3,087
		  1991 – 3,055

1945–1990 European and American politics and policies dominated by the 'Cold War' with Russia	1952– Queen Elizabeth II	
1973 Following a referendum, Great Britain joined the European Community		1977 Mrs Helga Blow
		1987 Detmar Blow
1989–1991 Collapse of Communist governments		

Church, Buildings, Roads, Landscape

1933–1985
Gyde Orphanage run by National Childrens' Homes

1934
Roman Catholic Church built

1941
Bell Hotel and Roman Catholic Church destroyed in air raid

1945 onwards
Many new houses built in the village, notably in the Castle Hale area, in Lower Washwell. The Croft, Randalls Field, Hyett Close, Brookhouse Mill and The Park

1946
The Plantation presented to the village in memory of Francis Hyett and William H. Hyett

1956
Roman Catholic Church restored

1969 New Church porch built

1970 Star Inn closed

1971
New Surgery in Gloucester Street

1973–1978
School moved from old National School building to the Croft

1978
Town Hall modernised

1981
Broadham Fields sports ground brought into use

1984
Reconstruction of Rococo Garden at Painswick House started

1993 Three new Church bells installed

Village Life and Events

1938
First Arts and Crafts exhibition

1941
Two evacuees killed in air raid

c.1942
The Painswick 'War Book' (in the Imperial War Museum) tells us that, for emergencies, the village had a megaphone, eleven horses, sixteen wheelbarrows and seven shotguns (among other items) but, better than that, there were about twenty-five to thirty volunteers in the Home Guard and Fire Brigade

1943
American Army camp in Painswick Park. Lord Dickinson (1st Baron) died

1945
W. St Clair Baddeley died

1977
Queen Elizabeth's Jubilee party in the village

1981
Late spring snowfall severely damaged the yew trees

Country Branch of the Alexandra Hospital
FOR CHILDREN WITH HIP DISEASE,
PAINSWICK.
OPEN TO VISITORS FROM 2 P.M. TO 5 P.M. DAILY.

Contributions towards the rent, and in support of the Painswick Cot,
FARTHINGS, OLD TRINKETS, AND "RUMMAGE" OF ALL KINDS,
thankfully received by Miss Thorold, Supt.

ESTABLISHED 1832.

Walter Henry Burdock,
BUILDER, PLUMBER, GLAZIER,
PAINTER, GAS FITTER,
General House Decorator, &c.,
PAINSWICK.

Hydraulic Rams, Deep-well Pumps, Beer Engines, Hot and Cold Water and Steam Fittings, and Bell-hangings. Writing, Graining, Marbling. A choice selection of Paper-hangings of the newest designs, from 3d. per piece, always in Stock. Patent welded-iron Tubes and Fittings for Gas, Steam, and Water, at Makers' prices. Agent for the Atlas Assurance Company.

C. FINCH,
BUILDER & UNDERTAKER,
PAINSWICK BUILDING AND JOINERY WORKS,
New St., Painswick

Contracts given for House Repairs in General. Venetian, Wire, and other Blinds to Order.

"The Falcon," Painswick.
FAMILY & COMMERCIAL HOTEL.
PRIVATE SUITES OF APARTMENTS.
(TERMS ON APPLICATION.)
TENNIS AND CROQUET LAWNS.
POSTING AND LIVERY STABLES.

Landaus, Broughams, Victorias, Wagonettes, Pony Carriages, and Dog Carts on hire.

J. H. WESTCOTT, Proprietor.

The Painswick Dairy Co.
MILK SUPPLIED TWICE DAILY

Butter, Cream, and Cream Cheese.

Eggs, Poultry, and Rabbits.

The Verlands Gardens.
FRUIT, FLOWERS, AND VEGETABLES
Always on Sale at Market Prices.

Flowering Plants for the Embellishment of Rooms.
FERNS, PALMS, &C.
Choice Flower and Vegetable Seeds and Plants. Bedding Stuff. Advice given to Customers.

APPLY MR. J. RUSSELL.

THE VERLANDS, PAINSWICK.
SUPERIOR BOARD, RESIDENCE, OR APARTMENTS
IN CHARMING HOUSE.

Large Garden. Shady Walks. Tennis and Croquet Lawns. Golf Links quite near.

Bath Room (H. and C.). Every Modern Convenience and Home Comforts.

HIGHEST REFERENCES.

APPLY MRS. RUSSELL.

Parish magazine 1903

GLOSSARY

(There are many different forms of spelling of all these terms)

Caliver: a light musket

Clipping (y-cleping) the Church: an ancient custom revived and kept annually at the Feast of the Blessed Virgin Mary, the patron saint. Children carrying posies circle the church, holding hands, and sing the Clipping Hymn. [NB—nothing to do with the clipping of the churchyard yews!]

Cotswold: Cote = a sheepfold; Wold = a bare hill
The author has found at least twenty different spellings of the name from c.1300 onwards

Englishry: of English nationality

Knap(p): 1. Crest of a hill
    2. Steep road or lane
    3. Possibly a place where flints were exchanged—derived from 'to knap' or break flints with a hammer

Land holdings—
  Copyhold(er): Land tenure as recorded in manorial records, a copy of which was given to the tenant
  Demesne land: the 'Home Farm' on the manorial estate
  Manor: a wide-ranging term. We would now call a manor a feudal estate. The principal building on it was the Manor House, originally the dwelling place of the Saxon Thane or the Norman Lord of the Manor
  Tenants: [All these terms are imprecise]
    A bordar (smallholder, or sometimes a cottager) held about 1 to 10 acres
    A cottager held land by cottier-tenure, the letting of a strip or strips of land by competition

[55]

Land holdings *cont.*
    Radknights: 'riding men' who served the Lord of the Manor as escorts or carried out special duties as required
    A serf held perhaps 1 acre
    A villein usually held a full virgate (30 acres)

Land measurements and terms—
    Bovate (half yard) = about 15 acres
    Carucate (caruca: a plough team): The area of land a plough team could cover in a year, equal to about 4 virgates
    Farendels (quarter yard) = about 7½ acres
    Frith: a wood (Saxon)
    Ham(m): enclosed pasture. The area of the village along Edge Road was known as The Ham(m)
    Ham(m)-butts:
        (1) the abutments (strips of land) 'abutting' the Lord's land
        (2) butts – a suitable area set aside for archery practice
    Hide: 2 to 4 virgates
    Homadge (homage): a tithing
    Hundred (or Danish wapentake): nominally consisted of a hundred hides, a hide (about 120 acres) being the area sufficient to support a family for a year. The estimated wealth of each 'hundred' was used as the basis for calculating tax. Originally, each hundred had an 'open' court for the settlement of private disputes.
    Leasow: a meadow or pasture
    Messuage: dwelling
    Mundies (eighth yard-land) = about 4 acres
    Pannage: payment for, or right of, pasturage for pigs
    Shag/shaw: coppice or thicket
    Vatch: a messuage (dwelling) and field
    Virgate (yard-land) = about 30 acres
    Worth: enclosed homestead

Legal terms—
    Advowson: the right to choose the clergy
    Court Leet: yearly or ½-yearly court of record held by the Lord of the Manor
    Fee (simple): to hold land as absolute property
    Feu: perpetual lease at fixed rent
    Free-bench: on her husband's death, a widow was 'admitted' to her 'free bench', i.e. one-third of the annual value of the tenancy rent on payment of one penny

Free-warren: the right to catch rabbits without payment to a landowner

Heriot(t): Tribute of best live beast, or 'dead' chattel, or money payment to Lord of the Manor, on death of tenant

Rose-lands: let at annual rent of one red rose

Seized of: having legal possession of

View of Frank-pledge: the duty of a Sheriff or Steward of the Manor to ensure that the law was enforced, especially by the 'tithingman' (see below) who stood as pledge or surety for criminals in their Tithing

Mark: unit of value—13s./4d.—introduced by the Danes. There was no coin of this value

Obulus: half penny coin

Painswick: According to Baddeley, it was recorded in 1888 that there were no less than thirty-three different spellings of the village name

Paradise: origin of the name obscure. Baddeley conjectures it may be from grains of paradise (possibly maize) imported from Tripoli in the fifteenth century and perhaps grown on the demesne land below the Beacon

Pennig, penning: penny (Old English)

Pyoner: pioneer: a foot soldier who travelled ahead of an army to prepare roads and bridges

Senechal: Steward of the Manor

Tithing: The village was divided into four areas known as tithings, each area in turn being divided into groups of ten householders living near together. The head 'tithingman' was responsible for the peaceable behaviour of his neighbours. (See 'View of Frank-pledge' above)

Wife-rip, child-rip: the amount of cereal or hay that a woman or child could reap in a given time

CORNER HOUSE. CHELTENHAM ROAD & GLOUCESTER ST. **A. JONES,** Family Grocer, Baker, & Mealman. Dealer in all kinds of Glass, China, & Earthenware. GOOD STOCK TO SELECT FROM.	**EDUCATIONAL.** **MISS BURDOCK,** Teacher of the Pianoforte & Singing, COTTESWOLD HOUSE, **PAINSWICK.** STUDENTS PREPARED FOR EXAMINATIONS.
J. RADFORD, *Linen Draper,* **HOSIER AND HABERDASHER,** **PAINSWICK.**	**J. E. WARNER,** *FAMILY GROCER,* **Wine and Spirit Merchant,** CANTON HOUSE, NEW STREET, **PAINSWICK.**
DOIDGE & HORLICK, The People's Drapers, Hosiers, AND OUTFITTERS, LONDON HOUSE, GLOUCESTER STREET, PAINSWICK. *Agents for*—Pullar's Dye Works, Perth; The Registered Unrivalled Ceylon Teas; Bradbury's and Singer's Sewing Machines; and The Queen Fire and Life Insurance Company. Men's and Boys' Suits, or Single Garments, made to Order or from Stock. *Dressmaking and Millinery Executed on the Premises.*	**PIANOFORTE.** **MISS FOWLER,** Certificated Pianist, Three years Teacher at Conservatorium (Germany), is prepared to receive Pupils. TECHNIQUE AND THEORY THOROUGHLY TAUGHT. Terms on application to Belmont House, Painswick. *N.B.*—Lessons in German also given.
H. W. Spring & Son, *PAINSWICK AND STROUD.* **Auctioneers and Timber Valuers,** AND VALUERS FOR ESTATE DUTY. Agents to The Sun Fire and Life Offices.	**G. W. BIRT,** Pound House, Gloucester Street, **PAINSWICK.** AGENT FOR THE "SUN" CYCLES. Two years guarantee with "Sun" Cycles. Tyre Repairers to the trade. Old tyres re-rubbered, re-lined, and turned out as new. All tyre work guaranteed. New Machines built to order, and guaranteed. Easy terms arranged for. Free wheels and back-pedalling brakes fitted at lowest prices. High-class enamelling, plating, &c. Cycles lent on hire.

Parish magazine 1903

BIBLIOGRAPHY

Atkins, Sir Robert: *The Ancient and Present State of Glostershire* (1712)

Baddeley, W. St Clair: *History of the Church of St Mary, Painswick* (1902)

Baddeley, W. St Clair: *A Cotteswold Manor being the History of Painswick* (1907, 1929, 1980 Editions: Alan Sutton Publishing Ltd, Stroud)

Domesday Book

Finberg, H. P. R.: *Gloucestershire, An Illustrated Essay on the History of the Landscape* (1955: Hodder and Stoughton)

Gloucestershire and North Avon Catholic History Society (1990)

Greensted, Mary: *The Arts and Crafts Movement in the Cotswolds* (1993: Alan Sutton Publishing Ltd, Stroud)

Heighway, Carolyn: *Anglo Saxon Gloucestershire*

Hyett, Sir Francis: *Glimpses of the History of Painswick* (1928, 1957 Editions: British Publishing Co, Gloucester)

McWhirr, Alan: *Roman Gloucestershire* (1986: Alan Sutton Publishing Ltd, Stroud)

Margetson, Stella: *Stage Coaching, 'Journey by Stages'* (1967)

Origo, Iris: *The Merchant of Prato* (1957: Jonathan Cape)

Painswick Parish Magazine

Victoria County History of Gloucestershire, Vol 11

Wright, G. N.: *The Cotswolds* (1991: David and Charles Publishers plc)

INDEX

Abbot of Gloucester, 16, 33
Advertisements, 43, 44, 45, 47
Advowson, 56
Agincourt, battle of, 32
Agriculture: importance in village life, 15, 26, 29, 45
Air raids, 53
Alfred, King of Wessex, 25, 27
American Army Camp, 53
Ankaret (Talbot), 32
Architecture of the village, 17, 48
Arkright, Richard, 44
Armada, Spanish, 38
Arts and Crafts Exhibition, 53
Arts and Crafts Movement, 17, 48
Assembly Rooms, 47
Athelstan, King, 27
Avignon, 13

Baddeley, W. St Clair, 9, 11, 12, 14, 51, 53
Baker, Charles, 47
Bannockburn, 32
Baptists, 45
Barnet Street (Gloucester Street), 35, 43
Barnsley, Sydney, 18
Barron, Phyllis, 18
Bathhouse, 18
Bath, 25, 27
Beacon, The, 19, 25, 28, 31
Beacon House, 45

Bell Hotel, 53
Bell ringers, Society of, 41, 51
Bembo (typeface), 64
Berkeley Castle, 14, 32
Berkeley family, 16, 33, 35
Beverstone Castle, 28
Bill of Rights, 40
Bisley, 25
Bisley Hundred, 29, 35
Bisley Street (High Street), 33, 35, 45
Black Death, 16, 32
Blow, Detmar I, 18
Blow, Detmar II, 50
Blow, Detmar III, 52
Blow, Mrs Helga, 52
Blow, Jonathan, 52
Boleyn, Anne, 37
Bordars, 55
Boundary adjustment, 51
Bovate, 56
Bristol, Siege of, 19, 40
Broadham Fields, 53
Brookhouse Mill, 33, 45, 49
Bruce, Robert, 32
Bryan, John, 43, 44
Bulcross (Bulls Cross), 39
Burdock & Co., 47
Burdock, Walter, 51
Burford, 16
Butt Green, 43

Caliver, 55

Canton Acre, 51
Canute (Cnut), King, 27
Cap Mill, 39
Carucate, 56
Castle Godwin, 28
Castle Hale, 29, 31, 33, 35, 37, 39, 47, 49
Cemetery, 49
Charles I, 18
Charters, Village, 31, 33
Chedworth, 25
Cheltenham, 19
Child-rip, 57
Chur, The, 33
Church building, 26, 33, 35, 37, 41, 43, 49, 53
Cirencester (Corinium), 16, 19, 25, 27, 40
Civil War, 18, 19, 40, 41
Clement VI, Pope, 13
Clipping Ceremony, 51
Cloth (and wool) trade, 15, 16, 33, 40, 45, 47, 49
Coinage, 30, 34
Cold War, 52
Colophon, 64
Columbus, Christopher, 34
Communism, 52
Comyn, Elizabeth, 32
Congregationalists, 41, 43, 45
Convicts, 47
Copyholders, 55
Coltswold (spellings), 33, 55

[60]

Cottager, 55
Court House, 19, 39
Court Leet, 56
Crécy, Battle of, 13, 32
Crimean War, 48
Cromwell, Thomas, Earl of Essex, 14, 36
Croome, A. C. M., 48
Croome, Thomas, 44
Croome, T. M., 46, 48
Crusades, 28
Currency, 30, 57
Curtis Green, W., 18
Customs of the Manor, 13, 14, 34, 40, 46

Damsel(l) family, 33
Damsells Mill, 41
Danes, 25
Dell Farm, 41
Demesne-lands, 55
Dickinson, Lord (1st Baron), 53
Dispensers, The, 32
Dissolution of the Monasteries, 36
Domesday Book, 12, 14, 26, 28, 29
Drake, Sir Francis, 38
Dudley, Sir Edmund, 34
Duntisbourne Rous, 26
Dursley, 16
Dutton, Sir Ralph, 19, 38, 40
Dyrham, battle of, 25, 27

Edge (Egge) (tithing), 18, 29, 37, 41
Edge parish, 49
Edward the Confessor, 27, 28
Edward the Elder, 27
Egbert, 27
Elizabeth, Countess of Devon, 34
Elkstone, 26
Emigrants, 47
Enclosure Acts, 17, 40, 43
Englishry, 55
Ernisi (Earnsige), Thane of Bisley, 12, 28

European Community, 52

Falcon Inn, 37, 43
Farendels, 56
Fee, 56
Feu, 56
Fitzjohn, Agnes, 13, 30
Fitzjohn, Cecilia, 28
Fitzjohn, Pain, 12, 28
Flanesford, Priory of, 13, 32, 33
Flemish weavers, 16
Free-bench, 56
Free-warren, 57
French Revolution, 44
French wars, 44
Friends, Society of, 41, 43
Frith Wood, 20, 39, 43

Gallows, the, 37, 39
Gardner, Thomas, 39
George III, visit to Painswick, 45
George Inn, 41
Gill, Eric, 18
Gimson, Ernest, 18
Glendower, Owen, 32
Gloucester (Glevum), 25, 27
Gloucester, Bishopric of, 36
Gloucester, siege of, 19, 41
Gloucester Street, 35, 43
Gloucestershire Guild of Craftsmen, Exhibitions, 18, 53
Godwin, Earl, 28
Godwin of Wyke, 31
Golf Course, 49
Great Fire of London, 40
Gunpowder Plot, 38
Gyde, Alms Houses, 18, 51
   Trustees, 49
   Orphanage, 18, 51, 53
Gyde, Edwin, 49, 51
Gyde, Frederick (Trust), 49
Gyde, John, 20

Ham (hamm), 56
Hambutts, 35
Hambutts House, 18

Hargreaves, James, 44
Hereford, Earl of, 28
Herings, 43
Heriot(t), 57
Hide, 56
High Street (Bisley Street), 35, 45
Hilles, 18
Homadge (homage), 56
Home Guard, 53
Hooper, Bishop, 36
Horsepools, 35
House building (modern), 51, 53
Hundreds, 25, 56
Hwicce (Kingdom of the), 27
Hyett, Charles, 43
Hyett, Sir Francis, 9, 11, 12, 47, 51
Hyett, William H., 47

Ifold, villa, 25
Industrial Age and Revolution, 18
Institute, village, 18, 51

Jeffrey, S., 41
Jenner, Edward, 42
Jeringham, family, 14, 36
   Sir Francis, 40
   Sir George, 42, 44
   Sir Henry I, 36
   Sir Henry II, 38
   Sir Henry III, 38
   Sir Henry IV, 40
   Sir John, 42
   Sir William, 44
Joan of Arc, 13

Kings Mill, 37
Kingston, Sir Anthony, 14, 19, 36, 37
Kingston, Sir William, 14, 36
Knap(p), 55

Laci family, 12
Laci, Hugh de, 28
Laci, Roger de, 28
Laci, Walter de, 28

[61]

Lamp, The, 18
Land holdings, 55, 56
Land measurements, 56
Lanthony (Llantony) Prima, Abbey (Wales), 28
Lanthony (Llantony) Secunda, Priory (Gloucester), 29, 33, 36
Larcher, Dorothy, 18
Leasow, 56
Legal terms, 56, 57
Lisle, Edward Grey (3rd Viscount), 34
Lisle, John (4th Viscount), 14, 34
Lisle, Margaret, 34
Lisle, Thomas (2nd Viscount), 14, 34
Little Fleece, 18, 33
Lodge (Park), The, 18, 19, 31, 36, 37, 38, 42, 44
Lovedays, family, 31, 37
Lovedays Mill, 41
Ludlow, 12
Ludlowes, 33, 45
Lych-gate, 51
Lygon, Roger, 39

Magna Carta, 30
Malmesbury, 27
Manor, 55
Maps, Castle Hale, 41
Maps, Ordnance Survey, 46
Mark, 57
Market Hall, 39
Markets, weekly, 43
Mayenne, Walter de, 28
Mayflower, 38
Mercia, Kingdom of, 25
Messuage, 56
Methodist Chapel, 49
Montfort, Simon de, 30
Morris, William, 18
Motley, William, 39
Munchensi, Jaoan de, 30
Munchensi, Warine de I, 30
Munchensi, Warine de II, 13, 30

Munchensi, William de I, 30
Munchensi, William de II, 30
Mundies, 56

Napoleonic Wars, 16
New Drive, 51
New Hall, 35
New Street, 35
Nibley Green, 'battle' of, 14, 34, 35
Norman Conquest, 28, 31
Northleach, 16
Northumbria, 25

Oakley, Sir George, 18
Obulus, 57
Offa, King of Mercia, 27
Omnibuses, horse-drawn, 51
Omnibuses, motor, 51
Orleans, Siege of, 13

Painswick Hotel, 51
Painswick House, 43, 47
Painswick Mill, 41
Pannage, 56
Pans Lodge, 43
Paradise, 57
Paris, Matthew (of St Albans), 30
Parish Councils, 50
Park, The, 33
Parliament, 19, 30
Parliament at Gloucester, 32
Paynes-wyke, 29
Pembroke, Earl of, 13, 30, 32
Penny, 57
Pig Street, 47, 49
Pin trade, 49
Plantagenet, Arthur, Viscount Lisle, 34
Plantation, 53
Poitou, William de, 34
Police Station, 51
Population, 29, 33, 37, 39, 41, 43, 45, 46, 48, 53
Post Office building, 35
Printing, moveable type, 34

Public baths, 51
Public houses (beer shops), 47, 49
Punishments (Statutes), 31, 35, 37, 39, 41, 45
Pyoner, 57
Pytte, Thomas, 37, 39

Queen Elizabeth's Jubilee, 53

Radknights, 26, 56
Railways, 46, 48
Reform Acts, 46
Rioters, 47
Roads, 37, 45, 46
Robert of Normandy, 28
Roberts, Mary, 47
Rococo Garden, 43, 53
Rogers, William, 41
Roman Catholic Church, 53
Roman period, 25, 27
Rose-lands, 57
Royal Society, 40
Rupert, Prince, 19, 38
Russell Street, 49

Salmon's Mill, 38
Savings Bank, 45
Saxon invasions, 25, 27
Saxton, Christopher, 22, 39
Schools, 39, 43, 48, 49, 53
Seagrym's Mill, 13
Seaman, Edward, 41
Second World War, 49
Seddon, Rev. W., 51
Seized of, 57
Senechal, 57
Serf, 56
Severn/Thames Canal, 44
Shag (Shaw), 56
Sheephouse, 36, 37
Sheepscombe (Shepescombe) (tithing), 18, 29, 37, 41
Sheepscombe (village), 31, 37, 39, 47
Shrewsbury, Earl of, 13, 20, 34
Skinners Mill, 37

[62]

Speed, John, 23, 39
Spinning Jenny, 44
Spoonbed (Sponebed) (tithing), 18, 29, 37, 41
Stage coaches, 43, 44, 45, 47
Stamage, Thomas, 39
Stamage's Lane, 37, 39
Star Inn, 45, 53
St Augustine, 25, 27
St Peter's Abbey (Monastery), Gloucester, 27, 28, 36
St Peter's Abbey, Hereford, 28
Stock House, 39, 47
Stocks, The, 49
Stow on the Wold, 19, 40
Stroud, 35, 37, 48
Stroud-end (Strode-end) (tithing), 18, 29, 37, 41
Sunday Schools, 45
Surgery, 53

Talbot family, 35
Talbot, Ankaret, 32
    Gilbert (3rd Baron), 32
    Gilbert (5th Baron), 32
    John (6th Baron), Earl of Shrewsbury, 13, 20, 34
    Richard (2nd Baron), 13, 32
    Richard (4th Baron), 32

Tewkesbury, 19
Tibby Well (Towys Well, Tobyes Well), 39
Tocknell's Mill, 39
Tollgate, Barnet Street, 43, 45
Tombs, 45
Town Hall, 39, 51, 53
Trafalgar, Battle of, 44
Turnpike Acts, 42, 43, 45
Tuscan traders, 16
Twining, Thomas, 41
Twynings Mill, 41
Tyndale, William, 36

Union with Scotland, 42
Upper Washwell, 51

Valence, Ay(l)mer de, 13, 32
Valence, William de, 13, 30
Vasco da Gama, 36
Vatch, 56
Vicarage, 49, 51
Vicarage Street, 51
Victoria Street, 49
View of Frank-pledge, 57
Viking invasions, 25, 27
Villa, Roman, 25
Village services, drainage, electricity, etc., 49, 51, 53

Villein, 56
Virginia Company, 38
Virgate, 56

Wages, prices, 35, 39
Walpole, Sir Robert, 42
War Book, 53
Wars, effects on the village; memorials, 18, 19, 20
Wars of the Roses, 34
Waterloo, Battle of, 20, 44
Watt, James, 44
Wellington, Duke of, 20
Weobley, 12
Wesley, John, 43
Wesleyan Church, 45
Wessex, 25
Wick Street, 39, 43
Wick Street House, 41
Wicke, Wyke, Wykeham (Painswick), 29
Wife-rip, 57
Winchcombe, 26
Winter, Cornelius, 45
Wool trade, 15, 16, 33, 40, 45, 47, 49
Worth, 56
Wyke Pagani, 29

Yew trees, 45, 53

GLOUCESTER
TYPESETTING SERVICES

Bembo, the type in which this book is set, was one of the first of the old typefaces to be produced. It is a copy of a Roman typeface cut by Francesco Griffo for the Venetian printer Aldus Manutius and was first used in the production of a book, De Aetna, by a Cardinal Pietro Bembo, in 1495. The type was taken as a model by Claude Garamond (1480–1561), a very noted and influential French printer, who first used his adaptation about 1530.

These typefaces have been slightly modified from time to time by later printers, but they have remained popular ever since as two of the most elegant types available.

I love a little bit of secret history.
DR JOHNSON